First
Facts

Rachel
Carson

A 4D BOOK

by Lisa M. Bolt Simons

CAPSTONE PRESS
a capstone imprint

Download the Capstone app!

- Ask an adult to download the Capstone 4D app.
- Scan the cover and stars inside the book for additional content.

When you scan a spread, you'll find fun extra stuff to go with this book! You can also find these things on the web at www.capstone4D.com using the password: carson.27735

First Facts are published by Capstone Press
1710 Roe Crest Drive, North Mankato, Minnesota 56003
www.mycapstone.com

Library of Congress Cataloging-in-Publication Data
Names: Simons, Lisa M. B., 1969– author.
Title: Rachel Carson : a 4D book / by Lisa M. Bolt Simons.
Description: North Mankato, Minnesota : an imprint of Capstone Press,[2019] |
Series: First facts. STEM scientists and inventors |
Audience: Age 6–9. | Includes index.
Identifiers: LCCN 2018001968 (print) | LCCN 2018004338 (ebook) | ISBN 9781543527810 (eBook PDF) | ISBN 9781543527735 (hardcover) | ISBN 9781543527773 (paperback)
Subjects: LCSH: Carson, Rachel, 1907–1964—Juvenile literature. | Biologists–United States—Biography—Juvenile literature. | Environmentalists—United States—Biography—Juvenile literature. | Science writers—United States—Biography—Juvenile literature.
Classification: LCC QH31.C33 (ebook) | LCC QH31.C33 S48 2019 (print) | DDC 570.92 [B] –dc23
LC record available at https://lccn.loc.gov/2018001968

Editorial Credits
Erika L. Shores and Jessica Server, editors; Charmaine Whitman, designer; Eric Gohl, media researcher; Laura Manthe, production specialist

Image Credits
Alamy: Randy Duchaine, 21, sjbooks, 17; AP Photo: 13; Getty Images: Alfred Eisenstaedt, 5, 15, Gado/JHU Sheridan Libraries, 9, Stock Montage, cover; Newscom: Everett Collection, 19; Shutterstock: A-Star, cover & interior (writing backgrounds), Oksancia, cover & interior (seaweed backgrounds); U.S. Fish and Wildlife Service: 11; Wikimedia: ccbarr, 7

Table of Contents

CHAPTER 3

A Science Writer

In 1936 Rachel became a biologist for the U.S. government. She researched and wrote about plants and animals that live in water. Rachel also published two books about the sea during that time. After 15 years, she quit her job to write full time.

FACT Rachel wrote short programs for the radio. Her scripts explained **marine** biology and work the government did.

Rachel spent years researching and writing about life in the Atlantic Ocean.

marine—living in the sea

Rachel published a third book called *The Edge of the Sea* in 1955. In her books, she wrote about ocean life. Rachel also wrote articles in magazines that taught people about nature. Many people read what she wrote. It made her famous.

Bestselling author

Rachel's second book was a bestseller for almost two years. It is called *The Sea Around Us* and was printed in 32 languages.

Rachel Carson (third from left) received a National Book Award for *The Sea Around Us* in 1952.

After years of research, Rachel discovered that pesticides damaged living things. She said spraying pesticides on farm crops did more than just kill pests. Rachel wrote about her findings in her book *Silent Spring*. It warned people about the need to care for the environment.

Rachel did research and wrote in her home office.

When Rachel's book came out, not everyone was happy. **Chemical** company owners were upset. They did not like that Rachel said pesticides were dangerous. Some people in government also disagreed with her. But many people had read her book. The environment was now a serious concern.

chemical—a substance used in or made by chemistry; pesticides and medicines are some of the things made with chemicals

A PENGUIN BOOK

Rachel Carson

'... what we have to face is not
an occasional dose of poison
which has accidentally got
into some article of food, but
a persistent and continuous
poisoning of the whole
human environment ...'

Silent Spring

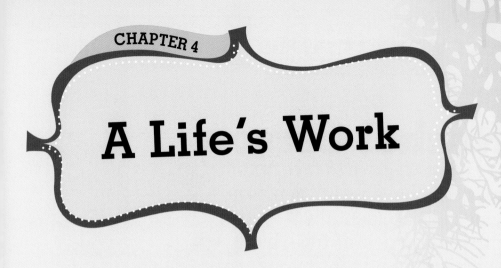

CHAPTER 4

A Life's Work

On April 3, 1963, a TV show featured Rachel and her work. About 15 million people watched the program. In June, Rachel spoke in front of **Congress**. She asked the government to make rules to help protect people and the environment from pesticides.

"The aim of science is to discover and **illuminate** truth."

Rachel Carson

Rachel speaking to Congress on June 4, 1963

Congress—the group of people who make laws for the United States

illuminate—to make known

Sadly, Rachel did not see the results of her life's work. She died from cancer on April 14, 1964. She was 56. But her work had changed people's minds. The need for clean water, land, and air was clear. In 1970 the government started the Environmental Protection Agency. Laws were passed. Rachel Carson helped change the world.

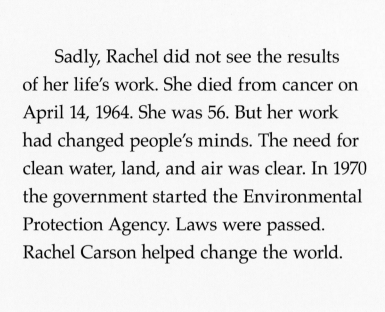

Award winner

Many groups awarded Rachel for her work. The National Audubon Society gave her a medal in 1963. The American Geographical Society also gave her a medal that year. After her death, Rachel was given the Presidential Medal of Freedom. This U.S. medal is the highest award given to a person not in the military.

The Rachel Carson National
Wildlife Refuge is in Maine.

Glossary

biology (by-AH-luh-jee)—the study of life and all living things

chemical (KE-muh-kuhl)—a substance used in or made by chemistry; pesticides and medicines are some of the things made with chemicals

concern (KUHN-surn)—a worry or a problem

Congress (KAHN-gruhs)—the group of people who make laws for the United States

environment (in-VY-ruhn-muhnt)—the natural world of the land, water, and air

explore (IK-splor)—to go searching or looking around

illuminate (i-LOO-muh-nayt)—to make known

marine (muh-REEN)—living in the sea

pesticide (PES-ti-side)— a poisonous chemical used to kill insects, rats, and fungi that can damage plants

publish (PUHB-lish)—to make and sell a book, magazine, newspaper, or any other printed material so that people can buy it

Read More

Hile, Lori. *Rachel Carson: Environmental Pioneer.* Chicago: Heinemann Library, 2015.

Heitkamp, Kristina Lyn. *Rachel Carson : Pioneering Environmental Activist.* New York: Rosen Publishing Group, 2018.

Rowell, Rebecca. *Rachel Carson Sparks the Environmental Movement.* Great Moments in Science. Minneapolis: Core Library, an imprint of Abdo Publishing, 2016.

Internet Sites

Use Facthound to find Internet sites related to this book.

Visit *www.facthound.com*

Just type in 9781543527735 and go!

Check out projects, games and lots more at
www.capstonekids.com

Critical Thinking Questions

1. How was Rachel able to combine her love of biology and writing?

2. Why does the last fact about Rachel's Presidential Medal of Freedom make her story even more important?

3. Why were chemical company owners angry at Rachel when she published *Silent Spring*?

Index